P9-DBJ-714

CYBER CRIME

by Colin Hynson

A+

Smart Apple Media

Published by Smart Apple Media
P.O. Box 3263, Mankato, Minnesota 56002

Printed in the United States of America at Corporate
Graphics, in North Mankato, Minnesota.

Published by arrangement with the Watts Publishing
Group LTD, London.

Library of Congress Cataloging-in-Publication Data
Hynson, Colin.
Cyber crime / Colin Hynson.
    p. cm. — (Inside crime)
Includes index.
  Summary: "Describes the crimes committed
  with computers over the Internet and various
  law enforcement agencies that fight cyber
  crimes. Includes real-life case studies and
  examples of crimes solved around the world"
  —Provided by publisher.
ISBN 978-1-59920-396-6 (library binding)
1. Computer crimes—Juvenile literature.
2. Computer crimes—Prevention—Juvenile
    literature. I. Title.
  HV6773.H96 2012
  364.16'8—dc22
                                    2010043232

1306
3-2011

9 8 7 6 5 4 3 2 1

Series editor: Jeremy Smith
Editors: Sarah Ridley and Julia Bird
Design: sprout.uk.com
Artworks: sprout.uk.com
Picture researcher: Diana Morris

Picture credits: Yuri Arcurs/Shutterstock: front
cover c, 16. John Birdsall/PAI: 17. CC. Some rights
reserved: 32 inset. Richard Clement/Reuters/
Corbis: 40. designalldone/istockphoto: 13b. Dennis
Guichard/Alamy: 27. Mark Harwood/Alamy: 20b.
Sutton-Hibbert/Rex Features: 41. Image Source/
Alamy: 8. Henrik Jonsson/istockphoto: 22. Chung
Sung-Jun/Getty Images: front cover t, 5. Michael
Jung/Shutterstock: 31. Yannis Kontos/Sygma/Corbis:
35t. Vitaly M/Shutterstock: 30. Tom Mihalek/AFP/
Getty Images: 21. Brian Minkoff, London Pixels.
CC.Some rights reserved: 25. Misty Dawn Photo/
Shutterstock: 11. MLG: 29. Jeff Morgan Technology/
Alamy: 20t. Olivier Morin/Getty Images: 33. Chuck
Nacke/Alamy: 39. Made Nagi/epa/Corbis: 10.
NATO Photos: 35b. Nikreates/Alamy: 26. Darko
Novakovic/Shutterstock: front cover t, 28. Masatoshi
Okauchi/Rex Features: 9. Fredrik Persson/AFP/
Getty Images: 32. Andy Rain/epa/Corbis: 14.
Markel Redondo/Getty Images: 34. Rex Features:
15. David Rubmeyer/Getty Images: 38. Alex Segre/
Rex Features: 24. Sony Pics/Everett/Rex Features:
23. Charles Sykes/Rex Features: 18. Ultra F/Getty
Images: 19. U.S. Navy/Getty Images: 36. Photo
provided by the US Secret Service/AP/ PAI: 37t. Nick
Ut/AP/PAI: 12. Alex Wong/Getty Images: 37b.

Every attempt has been made to clear copyright.
Should there be any inadvertent omission please
apply to the publisher for rectification.

CONTENTS

INSIDE PICTURE

The arrival of the Internet in homes, schools, and businesses has given everybody many opportunities to change the way that they live their lives. Online shopping, entertainment, and information has made the lives of many of us more varied and much easier. However, it is this very ease that has made the Internet a new gathering place for criminals and has created a new kind of crime: cyber crime.

Reporting Cyber Crime

It is very difficult to measure the amount of cyber crime that actually takes place around the world. There are several reasons why this difficulty exists. Many victims of cyber crime do not report what has happened to them to the police or may not even be aware that they have been a victim of cyber crime. Some businesses, such as banks, are reluctant to make it public that a cyber crime has been committed against them because of the bad publicity that would arise if they did.

◄ *In an age where most of us have access to the Internet, cyber crime is a growing danger.*

What Is Cyber Crime?

Cyber crime is any criminal activity that uses single computers, networks of computers, or the Internet. Some people also consider crimes that use mobile phones or PDAs (personal digital assistants or handheld computers) as cyber crimes. Many cyber crimes that are committed are crimes that have been around for a long time, but are now taking advantage of these new technologies. Fraud and copyright theft, for example, were problems before the arrival of computers, but with the rise of the Internet, it has become easier to commit these crimes and much harder for the police to catch the criminals. There are also some crimes that can only be committed using computer technology. Crimes such as hacking or denial-of-service attacks (see pages 10–13 and 28–29) are new criminal acts that would not happen if the computer technologies did not exist.

ON TARGET

The U.S. Internet Crime Complaint Center (IC3) gives the victims of cyber crime an easy-to-use reporting system that alerts government authorities of suspected criminal or civil violations. For law enforcement agencies at all levels, IC3 provides a central referral system for complaints involving Internet-related crimes.

The Extent of Cyber Crime

There have been some estimates of how many people have been victims of cyber crime. A 2009 report published by the Internet Crime Complaint Center (IC3), which is part of the United States Department of Justice, shows that they received more than 336,000 complaints about cyber crime in 2009. Nearly 44 percent of the complaints were deemed criminal and sent on to law enforcement agencies for investigation. Approximately $560 million was reported lost by victims of cyber crime. However, some research shows that as few as one in seven cyber crimes are reported.

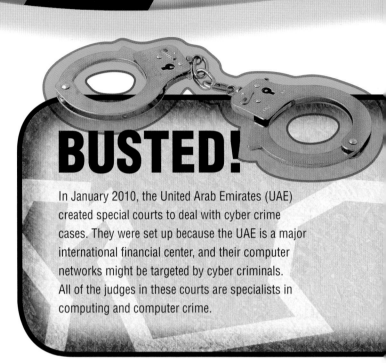

BUSTED!

In January 2010, the United Arab Emirates (UAE) created special courts to deal with cyber crime cases. They were set up because the UAE is a major international financial center, and their computer networks might be targeted by cyber criminals. All of the judges in these courts are specialists in computing and computer crime.

▶ *This is the computer system at the Earth Simulator Center, Yokohama, Japan. Cyber criminals do not just attack the vulnerable computers of individuals, but they will also target the computer systems used by governments and big businesses.*

HACKING

One of the crimes that has arisen as a result of the spread of computer technology is hacking. A hacker is somebody who gains unauthorized access to another computer system. Successful hackers can find secret information about individuals, businesses, or even governments. They can also change that information to spread confusion or create doubts about its reliability.

Different Hats

People who hack into computer systems have different reasons for doing so. Because of this, hackers have been divided into different groups.

White hat hackers: these people do not intend to commit a crime. They are looking for information or enjoy the challenge of getting into computers.

Black hat hackers: these hackers are sometimes called "crackers." They intend to commit a crime, such as fraud, or will take control of a web site and change the way that it looks.

Gray hat hackers: this group behaves somewhere between white hat and black hat hackers.

Hacktivists: (see page 35) similar to black hat hackers, except that they usually have a political motive for hacking.

▲ Indonesian students work on their computers to test the security of various computer systems during a regional hacking convention in 2007.

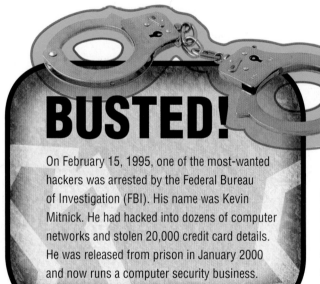

BUSTED!

On February 15, 1995, one of the most-wanted hackers was arrested by the Federal Bureau of Investigation (FBI). His name was Kevin Mitnick. He had hacked into dozens of computer networks and stolen 20,000 credit card details. He was released from prison in January 2000 and now runs a computer security business.

Hacking into Computers

There are various ways that hackers can get into a computer. It usually involves looking for a weakness in the security that surrounds a computer network. Once that weakness has been found, it becomes much easier to get into a computer network.

Even when computers are protected by passwords, hackers often find ways of discovering those passwords. Many hackers use "packet sniffers," software that watches for information being passed along computer networks, including passwords, and then sends that information to the hacker.

Protection from Hacking

Most computer systems have a firewall. A firewall is designed to protect a computer network from hackers being able to access that network. It does this by inspecting information either entering or leaving the network and only accepting it if it meets various security standards. Even firewalls have their weaknesses, though, and hackers can find their way through them. For this reason, hackers call firewalls "cottonwalls."

Cracking a password is not difficult in many cases. This is because many people use the same password for different purposes, do not often change them, and usually choose a password that has something to do with their lives (the name of a pet or their date of birth). For example, in September 2008, somebody was able to hack into the e-mail account of the Governor of Alaska and Vice-Presidential candidate Sarah Palin because her security question answers were easy to guess. They were her zip code, her date of birth, and the place where she first met her husband.

▶ *It was relatively easy for hackers to access Sarah Palin's e-mail account because her security details were easy for hackers to guess.*

CASE STUDY: GARY McKINNON

One of the most famous hacking cases involves a man from Britain named Gary McKinnon. He is wanted in the United States after he was accused of hacking into the computer networks of NASA, the United States Army, Navy, and Air Force, and the Department of Defense. His case is seen by many people as one in which the United States authorities are overreacting to a harmless white hat hacker.

FACT FILE

The United States authorities claim that McKinnon had:

- Deleted files from computers which shut down 2,000 U.S. Army computers for 24 hours

- Deleted files from U.S. Navy computers just days after the September 11th attacks in New York in 2001

- Cost the United States military $700,000

The Hacking Begins

In 2001, Gary McKinnon, using the name "Solo," started trying to hack into United States government computer networks. He discovered several computer networks that did not have adequate firewall or password protection and found a way into those computers. He claims that he was looking for evidence of Unidentified Flying Objects (UFOs) and that he believed that the United States government was hiding extraterrestrial technology that could provide free and non-polluting energy.

◀ *Gary McKinnon has Asperger's syndrome, a form of autism. His family feels he should not stand trial in the United States, as he will be unable to cope with the experience.*

The Pentagon is the headquarters of the U.S. Department of Defense. McKinnon successfully hacked into their computer system.

Arrested

Gary McKinnon was arrested by the British police in March 2002. It had been easy for the police and the military authorities in the United States to find out who he was because, unlike many hackers, McKinnon did not try to cover his tracks.

In 2005, American authorities began proceedings to have McKinnon extradited to the United States so he could be put on trial. He will be charged with hacking into government computers and with being a threat to the security of the United States.

Extradition Challenged

Since 2005, Gary McKinnon has tried to appeal against his extradition to the United States. He has argued that since any crime he might have committed took place in Britain, then he should be tried in Britain. He also thinks that he will not get a fair trial in the United States and that, if found guilty, he will face a heavier prison sentence because he is resisting the extradition. McKinnon has been diagnosed with a condition known as Asperger's syndrome. People with this condition often become so obsessed by something that they do not think about the effect of their actions on others.

McKinnon's family feels that his Asperger's condition makes him unfit to face trial in the United States. He has been unsuccessful in challenging the extradition. The British government has twice accepted that he should be sent to the United States for trial. The British High Court and the European Court of Human Rights have both stated that the extradition should go ahead. Further court cases are expected.

BUSTED!

The United States military authorities believe that McKinnon is not just a harmless hacker. A spokesman from the Pentagon stated: "This was not some harmless incident. He did very serious and deliberate damage to military and NASA computers and left silly and anti-American messages. All the evidence was that someone was staging a very serious attack on U.S. systems."

PHISHING

Hackers try to find information, such as passwords, by breaking into computer systems without the knowledge of the person using the computer. Criminals involved in phishing try to do the same thing, but they do it by fooling the user into revealing their details. They do this by e-mailing people or by contacting them on their telephone.

How Phishing Is Done

For most people, their experience of phishing comes through their e-mail. This kind of e-mail is sometimes called spam. Spam is unwanted e-mails that is trying to sell something. It is estimated that over 100 billion spam messages are sent every day and can account for over 90% of all e-mail received. Most spam is legal as long as the sender is trying to sell something legitimate. However, spam that is phishing is illegal because they attempt to defraud people.

BUSTED!

In 2004, the FBI launched a worldwide investigation into phishing attacks on a large financial institution. Named "Operation Cardkeeper," it involved working with police departments across Europe, especially in Poland and Romania. Agents from the FBI had to identify the criminals who were running a web-based business selling the bank and credit card details of phishing victims. It took over two years to gather all of the information before arrests could be made.

◀ Phishing e-mails will often lead people to a web site that looks normal and legitimate, but is actually fraudulent. Then users are duped into giving away their login and password details.

Phishing e-mail usually tries to get access to a person's financial details by pretending to be from a legitimate business, such as a bank. The message will say that there is some sort of problem with their bank account and then provide a link to a web site so that the problem can be solved.

Fake Web Sites

In many phishing scams, when people click on the link in an e-mail, they are sent to a web site that looks exactly like the web site of their bank but is in fact a fake web site. If the person then types bank account details on the fake site, the phisher can access the real bank account and take money out of that account. Once the phishers have somebody's details, they can also steal their identity and use it to set up other bank accounts, claim social security, or even apply for passports.

The Cost of Phishing

If somebody becomes a victim of a phishing attack and loses money, then the bank will usually repay the money. This means that it is the banks who are most concerned about the extent of phishing that is taking place. Banks are sometimes reluctant to make it public that their customers have fallen victim to phishing because of the bad publicity that might come with it. However, it was estimated that in 2008 in the United States alone, phishing attacks cost banks and other financial institutions about $3 billion.

BUSTED!

In October 2009, American and Egyptian police worked together to bust a phishing scam that has been described as the largest cyber crime investigation ever. The investigation was named Operation Phish Phry (see photo below). Phishers based in Egypt managed to get bank account details of thousands of Americans. After a two-year investigation, police in both countries arrested over 100 people.

▲ At a press conference held in November 2009, FBI officials announced the success of Operation Phish Phry (see BUSTED! box).

CYBERBULLYING

Many children and young people have been the victims of bullying either at school or elsewhere. In recent years, parents and teachers have become concerned about a new kind of bullying called cyberbullying. This uses web sites, e-mails, and cell phones to bully somebody and to encourage other people to take part in the bullying.

Types of Cyberbullying

There are many different ways in which people can be cyberbullied. One of the most common ways is to send hurtful text messages on cell phones. However, the Internet is increasingly being used as a way of attacking people. Blogs and social networking sites, such as Bebo, MySpace, and Facebook, have been used to bully particular individuals. Embarrassing photographs can be posted on web sites or sent around a group of people on cell phones. Along with photographs, personal details such as a person's name, e-mail address, or phone number can also be put on a web site, and viewers are encouraged to send the victim messages. Some victims have been known to receive hundreds of text and e-mail messages every day.

The Extent of Cyberbullying

Just like physical bullies, cyberbullies rely on the silence of their victims, so it is very difficult to know how many young people have been cyberbullied. In 2006, an organization in the United States called i-SAFE polled 1,500 children between ages 9 and 16 and asked them questions about cyberbullying. It reported that:

42%	said that they have been bullied online
25%	said that they had been bullied online more than once
21%	said that they had received hurtful e-mail
58%	had not told any adults about the cyberbullying

◀ *Social networking sites are open to cyberbullying because the bullies can stay anonymous.*

BUSTED!

After the suicide of 13-year-old Megan Meier in Missouri in 2006, three people were arrested. They had created a false identity of a teenage boy on MySpace and used it to repeatedly bully Meier, a girl in their neighborhood. In the end, the judge ruled that they could not be charged with causing her death because of a lack of laws against cyberbullying. However, the leader was found guilty of some lesser charges of computer fraud. Since this case ended, several U.S. states have created laws against cyberbullying.

▼ Features on cell phones such as e-mail, video, and texting mean that cyberbullies can attack their victims in lots of different ways, and they can also share what they have done with many other people.

The Price of Cyberbullying

Newspapers and television news have produced reports on young people who have harmed themselves or even attempted suicide because of cyberbullying. In January 2009, a 15-year-old girl in Macclesfield, England, took an overdose of pills and was later found dead by her parents. It was discovered that not only was she being bullied at school, but fellow students were leaving messages about her on Bebo.

CYBERSTALKING

Cyberbullies and cyberstalkers both use the Internet and other electronic means to send unwanted messages to their victims. However, cyberstalkers also use the Internet to stalk their victims.

What is Cyberstalking?

Many people have been the victims of the crime of stalking. Stalking is a term used when somebody is receiving unwanted attention from another person. The victim may be continually telephoned or even followed by a stalker. Sometimes the stalker wants to cause their victim harm, but more often the stalker may have feelings toward the victim and uses stalking as a way to get close to them. It is believed that five percent of all adults have been stalked.

Cyberstalkers use computer and cell phone technology to stalk a person, tracking their online activities. Just like cyberbullies, they leave messages on social networking sites, e-mail their victims, or even find out more about their victims by hacking into their computers.

▶ Because they are in the public eye, many celebrities, like American Idol *finalist Diana DeGarmo, find that they fall victim to stalkers.*

ON TARGET

Unlike cyberbullying, cyberstalking is illegal in many countries. In the United States, the Communications Decency Act of 1997 was changed in 2003 to include cyberstalking as an offense. On top of that, over 40 American states have passed their own laws that make cyberstalking illegal. Both Australia and Britain have also passed laws that make it illegal to cyberstalk somebody. These have usually been laws that cover all forms of stalking, including cyberstalking.

Celebrity Victims

Most victims of cyberstalking are just ordinary members of the public. However, celebrities can also become victims of cyberstalking. They can be stalked either by people who hate them and want to hurt them, or at the opposite extreme, by people who have become obsessed with them. In 2006, Diana DeGarmo, a finalist on the television series *American Idol*, reported that she was being cyberstalked by somebody who was threatening to blackmail her. An Australian woman was arrested after e-mailing and calling DeGarmo over 60 times a day. She had also hacked into DeGarmo's MySpace page and sent e-mails to DeGarmo's family and friends.

Grooming

Grooming is when an adult makes contact with young people on social networking sites and chat rooms. These adults often pretend that they are young people themselves. Their intention is to find out more details about the children they are in contact with and establish a relationship with them, online or offline. It can lead to face-to-face meetings and sometimes to unwanted sexual advances. In March 2010, a 33-year-old man named Peter Chapman was sent to prison for the murder of Ashleigh Hall, a 17-year-old girl. They had first come into contact through Facebook where he pretended to be only two years older than Ashleigh. They met in secret, where she was attacked and killed.

▶ *Many young people use chat rooms and social networking sites to keep in touch with their friends or to meet new people who share similar interests. There are fears that they may come into contact with older people who want to befriend them and do them harm.*

BUSTED!

Only three weeks after the state of California outlawed cyberstalking, the Los Angeles Police Department arrested a man who was cyberstalking a woman after she refused to go on a date with him. He posted messages on various web sites and chat rooms saying that she was looking for a boyfriend, and he gave out her address and telephone number online. He pleaded guilty to the crime of cyberstalking.

VIRUS ATTACKS

For many people, the main threat to the security of their computer is a computer virus. Computer viruses can infect an entire computer system and can cause unknown damage to a computer by destroying or even deleting information stored on that computer. It costs a lot of money to repair the damage done by viruses, which is why creating and distributing a computer virus is a cyber crime.

▲ An expert repairs a complicated computer system. A virus attack on a computer system often means that all the computers linked to the system have to be turned off while repairs are done.

What Is a Virus?

A computer virus is a small piece of software that attaches itself to another piece of software on a computer, such as word-processing or spreadsheet software. Whenever that software is run, the virus can take control of the software and change it in some way. It is called a virus because, like biological viruses, it can copy itself and then go on to infect other computers. It does this either by spreading itself around a computer network or by sending the virus as an attachment to an e-mail or as part of a web site. If it is part of an e-mail, then the virus can read the address book in the e-mail software and then send itself to those addresses, all without the computer user's knowledge.

▼ This is a biological virus under the microscope. Computer viruses work in the same way as biological viruses, but they take over a computer rather than the cells of a human body.

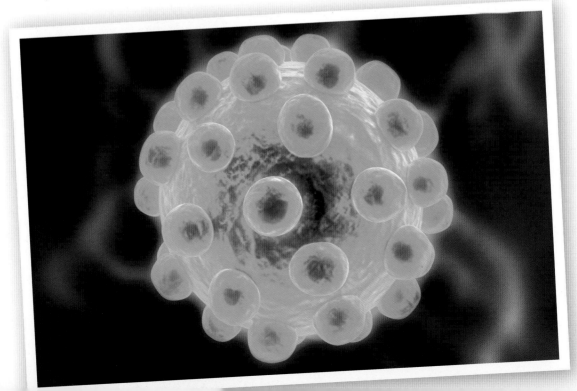

BUSTED!

Because viruses can spread around the world in less than a day, it is very difficult to catch virus writers. However, the creators of the Melissa and ILOVEYOU viruses (see below) have been arrested, although many other writers are still free. In 2003, Microsoft was so concerned about the impact of viruses on computers around the world that it offered a cash reward to anybody who could identify the creators of various viruses.

Virus Attacks

In March 1999, a virus called Melissa forced several companies, including Microsoft, to shut down their e-mail services. The original virus was not designed to cause harm, but it did clog up e-mail accounts as it replicated itself. The later version of Melissa caused problems as it deleted various files on computers.

The ILOVEYOU virus originated in the Philippines in May 2000 and started to delete files on any computer that it infected. It spread itself as an e-mail attachment and was around the world in less than a day. The virus caused the Pentagon and the CIA to shut down their e-mail systems until the virus was cleared. Many large companies were also badly affected by ILOVEYOU.

▶ *The Melissa virus was created by David Smith. He was arrested in April 1999, just a week after the virus first appeared. He was sentenced to 20 months in prison, given a fine of $5,000, and ordered not to use the Internet without permission.*

The Cost of Virus Attacks

People create viruses for various reasons. Many of them are created by individuals who simply want the thrill of knowing that something that they made is causing difficulties. However, some virus writers do work with other cyber criminals, such as hackers.

Like many other cyber crimes, it is hard to define the cost of a virus attack. This is usually because it is hard to calculate. For instance, if the computer network of a business is infected with a virus then the whole network will have to be shut down until the virus is removed and any damage repaired. Any business that they might have conducted during this time will be lost. Individual viruses can cause millions of dollars of damage to businesses worldwide.

MALWARE

There are some pieces of software that are often confused with computer viruses because they can cause damage to a computer. However, they do not copy themselves, and the damage that they do is often unseen by computer users. These pieces of software are often called malware. Spyware, adware, and trojan horses are different kinds of malware.

BUSTED!

In May 2008, a computer hacker named Albert Gonzales was arrested after police found evidence that he had masterminded one of the largest computer frauds in history. He is suspected of using a piece of malware to steal the details of over 170 million credit card owners, which he then sold to criminal gangs.

What Is Malware?

Malware, short for malicious software, is the name for any software or file that installs itself onto someone's computer without their permission. It often downloads onto a computer in the same way as a computer virus. Once there, it can allow cyber criminals to gain information such as passwords, bank account numbers, and other forms of identity. Malware can find this

▶ One of the problems that police have with tracing the creators of malware is that there is no single place where the crime has been committed. Every computer that is infected with malware becomes a crime scene.

CRIME SCENE
CROSS
DO NOT

information in a number of ways. Some malware can record the keystrokes made on a keyboard and then send them back to the malware creator. It can redirect the user from one web site to another or even take screen shots and send that information back as well. Some malware software uses infected computers to send out spam e-mail.

Types of Malware

A trojan horse, another type of malware, works by pretending to be a piece of software that the user will find useful. In 1999, a trojan horse offered an upgrade to Internet Explorer, but if it was installed, the creator of the trojan horse could take control of the victim's computer. Spyware keeps track of how a computer is being used and then sends that information back to the spyware creator. Adware is a piece of software that, if downloaded, automatically displays advertisements on a computer. It can also track which web sites a computer user visits and send that information back to the creator. They can then decide what kind of advertisements to send that user.

The Cost of Malware

Malware costs businesses around the world billions of dollars every year. This is because malware usually makes computers run more slowly, and they do not work as well. It also costs money to buy the software needed to combat malware, and occasionally a computer network has to be closed down so that the malware can be removed properly.

ON TARGET

In October 2009, police warned Michael Jackson fans that they were being targeted by a new piece of malware. Some of the video downloads of Michael Jackson's last single "This Is It" on the web had malware hidden inside them. Once the video was on a computer, then so was that malware, which stole security passwords and sent them back to cyber criminals.

▶ The death of Michael Jackson in June 2009 created much interest in "This Is It," his last song and the name for a series of concerts in London. The interest alerted cyber criminals of the opportunity to use malware to commit identity theft.

SOCIAL NETWORKING SITES

For many people, one of the most enjoyable ways of using the Internet is on social networking sites such as Facebook, Twitter, MySpace, Bebo, and Second Life. These web sites allow people to keep in touch with friends and colleagues around the world and to share information with them. It is this information that makes them a target for cyber criminals.

Site Vulnerabilities

Many people who use social networking sites give away a lot of details about themselves. These can include e-mail addresses, phone numbers, and birthdays. If cyber criminals can access these details, then those people could become victims of identity theft or even allow hackers access to their bank details. It is also easy for cyber criminals to pretend to be somebody else on a social networking site and then gather information from people who have been fooled into thinking they are communicating with the person being impersonated.

ON TARGET

Police can use social networking sites to look for known criminals. They can do this by searching for profiles set up by criminals who often use their real names or can be traced through their e-mail addresses. The moment the criminal uses the web site, it becomes easier to trace them. The people who run the web sites cooperate with the police in catching criminals who use their sites.

▶ *Many cell phones have Internet access. People can use these phones to keep in touch with their friends on social networking sites. However, hackers can hack into cell phones and steal personal information that is stored on the phones.*

► *British writer, actor, and comedian Stephen Fry has many followers on Twitter, and he was also a victim of a hacking attack on Twitter.*

There have been reports of hackers successfully managing to get into social networking sites and then passing user details to cyber criminals. In 2009, a user of Facebook had her profile hacked into. A message that seemed to come from her was sent to her friends, asking them for money to help her return home after a robbery. At least one person sent some money, but it ended up in the pockets of the hackers.

Fake Social Networks

In September 2009, several users of Twitter received a message that contained a link to what appeared to be another part of Twitter. If they clicked on it, they were taken to a web site where they were asked for their user name and password. It turned out to be a fake web site, and the cyber criminals who set it up were hoping to use the user names and passwords to gain access to other Twitter accounts. Twitter users were advised to change their passwords.

Second Life Crime

Second Life is a virtual world where people can create an "avatar" (an online personality) that can interact with other avatars. It has been a target for hackers. In November 2006, a virus attack called "gray goo" forced Second Life to close down for a short time. The virus slowed the whole site down to a crawl, irritating users.

BUSTED!

In October 2009, criminal Maxi Sopo was living in Mexico but was wanted in the United States for fraud. The police discovered that he was on Facebook and began to search through his friends. They discovered that one of Sopo's friends used to work for the U.S. Department of Justice. They contacted him, and with his help, they traced Sopo to Mexico and arrested him.

FRAUDULENT WEB SITES

Many fake web sites exist without the need for phishing. If people are looking for products on the Internet, then they may find a web site that promises to supply a service but does not deliver anything. This can range from sites selling tickets, music, and clothes to computer games and other goods.

Searching for Goods

Online shopping has grown at an extraordinary rate over the past few years. In 2007, U.S. shoppers spent $126 billion online. By 2009, that figure had grown to $134 billion. Some experts now believe that up to half of all shopping will be done online by 2012. Online companies use encryption technology to protect people online. This technology scrambles information such as credit card details so that it cannot be read by hackers. Encryption means that it is nearly impossible for hackers to obtain any information from these web sites. This also means that cyber criminals will look for different ways to defraud people through web sites.

▲ Ugg boots were an incredibly popular fashion item. Many online shoppers have been disappointed when the boots they ordered online never arrived, or they received cheap imitations instead of the real Ugg boots.

Fake Sites

Cyber criminals have created web sites that imitate the sites of major companies in the hope that people will give their details to them after falling victim to a phishing attack. However, this is not the only way in which cyber criminals can use the Internet to steal money. It is fairly easy to set up a web site offering to sell goods or provide a service, take details from people who want to buy something, then simply disappear with the money. This is fraud, but because these web sites can operate from anywhere in the world, it is difficult to shut them down.

Tickets for Sporting Events

One of the biggest areas where cyber criminals can defraud people through fake web sites is by pretending to have tickets to major sporting events. Since 2008, there have been warnings of fake web sites that sell Super Bowl tickets. People who use these web sites either receive nothing or are sent fake tickets. In 2010, federal agents in the Miami, Florida area seized more than $150,000 in illegal Super Bowl tickets. Many had been for sale online. In Britain, fake web sites claim to sell tickets to big

BUSTED!

The E-Crime Unit, which is part of London's police department, closed down over 100 web sites that were claiming to sell tickets for the 2010 World Cup in South Africa. About 20 of these web sites were based in Britain. The rest were closed down with the assistance of police departments in Europe and Asia.

tennis and soccer games. Sports fans have been warned to take care when buying tickets online for the 2012 London Olympics.

▼ *Durban Stadium in South Africa was built to host the 2010 FIFA World Cup. Fake tickets for big events, such as this soccer game, flood the Internet before these events.*

DENIAL-OF-SERVICE ATTACKS

People who regularly use Internet services, such as e-mail and the web, rely on those services to be fast and reliable. If they become slow or do not seem to be working properly, this can create problems both for the people who run the Internet services and for their users. These services can be slowed down deliberately by using a denial-of-service attack.

How the Attacks Work

A denial-of-service attack works by bombarding a web site with so many requests to view the site that it cannot cope with the sudden and massive increase in demand. The web site will slow down so much that people using the site will have to wait for a long time to gain access. In some extreme cases, the site will be so overwhelmed by a denial-of-service attack that it simply stops working. Often, the computers taking part in these attacks are doing so without the owners' knowledge. Viruses take over the computers and use them for denial-of-service attacks. The infected computers are called "zombies."

BUSTED!

In November 2005, a British employee was arrested after sending his former employers over 5 million e-mail messages causing their server to crash. He was released since he did not change the computer system in any way. He could not be found guilty of a denial-of-service attack, as it did not become illegal in the UK until 2006.

◀ *A computer programmer spots a denial-of-service attack on a computer network.*

Why Do the Attacks Happen?

There is usually a criminal intention behind denial-of-service attacks. In 2004, the credit card firm Authorize.net received a blackmail demand saying that unless money was paid, it would become the victim of a denial-of-service attack. When the money was not paid, the attack began and it took several months before Authorize.net had normal service again.

These attacks are also a good way of hurting business rivals. In 2004, a businessman from Massachusetts was arrested after it was discovered that he was paying hackers in the United States and Britain to launch denial-of-service attacks on his competitors. They lost over $2 million from these attacks.

ON TARGET

As long ago as 1996, the United States created laws that make it illegal to launch denial-of-service attacks. People caught disrupting a business's computer networks can face felony charges and jail time if convicted. Other countries also have similar laws against denial-of-service attacks.

Web Attack

On August 6, 2009, Facebook, Twitter, and the blogging pages of Google came under a sustained denial-of-service attack. Google managed to survive the attack, but both Facebook and Twitter were brought down for several hours. It later became clear that the attacks came from Russia and were aimed at a Georgian blogger named "Cyxymu."

▲ The popularity of computer gaming makes the servers that supply the computer games a popular and easy target for denial-of-service attacks. Most of the attacks are organized by people who are unhappy with something in the game.

IDENTITY THEFT

Identity theft occurs when somebody gathers enough information about someone else that they can pretend to be that person. If they can find out a social security number or bank account details, then they can use that information to commit a crime, such as obtaining passports or getting a bank loan. Because so much of this information is held on computers, cyber criminals target them.

Ways of Stealing an Identity

There are various ways in which cyber criminals can steal somebody's identity. One of the most common is through phishing techniques. When people receive a phishing e-mail, they are given a link to a fake web site that looks genuine. On that site, they are asked for personal and financial details. Malware is another way in which identities can be stolen. For instance, if people type in their user name and password in order to access online banking, the malware will record all of that information and send it to the malware creator. Cyber criminals can also use information on social networking sites such as Facebook and Bebo. It is well known that people, particularly young people, are not careful about what information they put on these sites.

ON TARGET

Compared to the United States and Britain, identity theft is much more difficult in mainland European countries. This is mostly because people in many countries in Europe have a national ID card with a unique number. This number is normally carefully guarded and is only held by government computers. Private companies such as banks do not hold this information. European countries also have stricter laws about the kind of information that businesses can hold on their customers.

◀ Shopping online is usually safe and secure. However, sometimes cyber criminals are able to steal details of people's credit cards or bank accounts when they are used for online shopping by using malware or fake web sites.

► *False passports are one of the most valuable assets that can be created after an identity theft. These passports can be sold to drug smugglers, people traffickers, and other criminals.*

The Cost of Identity Theft

Governments and police forces around the world are becoming increasingly worried about identity theft. They believe that criminal gangs and even terrorists can use identity theft to give people working for them new identities. This makes them much harder to trace. A survey done in 2009 showed that more than 11.1 million people in the United States fell victim to identity theft. It is estimated that $54 billion was lost by people and business due to fraud and identity theft that year.

Decreases in Identity Theft

Although identity theft remains a major problem, there is some evidence that the number of reported identity thefts in most countries is beginning to decrease. Part of this is due to greater public awareness of the problem, as people are taking greater precautions. Anti-virus software and spam filters on e-mail accounts mean that phishing and malware are becoming less of an issue for computer users.

BUSTED!

In August 2008, the FBI cracked one of the largest cases of identity theft. Eleven people were arrested and charged with stealing over 40 million credit card details after hacking into the computer systems of several retail companies. Three of the 11 people charged were American, and the rest were from China and Europe. Police across Asia and Europe cooperated with the FBI in tracking them down.

CASE STUDY: PIRATE BAY

Sharing files across the Internet is not illegal in itself. There are many computer files that can be exchanged between users, and the exchange of these files is legal. However, the problem comes when the files being shared are pieces of music or films. Sharing these kinds of files breaks copyright law and is illegal. Two of the best-known music and film file sharers are Napster and Pirate Bay.

The Popularity of File Sharing

In 2004, CBS News polled 18- to 29-year-olds about file sharing. They found that over 70 percent of everybody in this age group illegally downloaded music and film files. Over half of them were unconcerned about the fact that this was against the law. It has been estimated that over 30 million Americans have downloaded at least one feature film from the Internet. Research done in 2008 showed that over 20 percent of all Europeans used BitTorrent web sites to download music (see page 33). Only 10 percent used legal sites such as iTunes. Many of them believe that they have the right to download music for free.

Pirate Bay Launched

In 2003, a Swedish organization called Piratbyran, launched a new web site called the Pirate Bay. It was a file-sharing site for music and video, and it soon became one of the most visited sites in the world. By February 2009, it had over 22 million regular users. This success has made it the target of police departments in Sweden and film and music companies around the world.

FACT FILE

In 2008, the International Olympic Committee (IOC) wrote a letter to the Swedish government asking them to prevent video clips of the Beijing Olympics being distributed through Pirate Bay. The IOC claimed that more than one million clips from the Olympics had been downloaded through Pirate Bay. The government could do nothing to help, and Pirate Bay temporarily renamed the site "Beijing Bay."

◀ Two of the founders of the Pirate Bay file-sharing web site wait to hear the result of the court case (see page 33) in February 2009.

▲ In June 2009, the Swedish Pirate Party won two seats in the European Parliamentary elections. The Pirate Party was founded by people who supported the Pirate Bay cause. It is now the third largest political party in Sweden.

How Pirate Bay Works

The people who run Pirate Bay claim that they are not breaking any copyright laws because the material that users download does not actually come from any Pirate Bay computer servers. Instead, it uses a technology known as BitTorrent. This works by acting as a kind of catalogue for other computers that hold illegally-held files. When somebody searches the Pirate Bay web site for a particular song or film file, they are then linked to the computer that does hold that file. Users can then download the file.

Pirate Bay Attacked

In May 2006, Swedish police raided the offices of Pirate Bay. Several truckloads of computer servers were taken away, the web site was closed down, and three people were arrested. With the help of volunteers around the world, the web site was up and running again in just three days. Since then, Pirate Bay has set up several servers in different locations so that it is almost impossible to close it down completely. In February 2009, the trial of the three men who started Pirate Bay began. They were charged with helping others to break copyright law. They were given a sentence of one year in prison and a fine that came to $4.2 million. In the same month, several record companies succeeded in having their material removed from Pirate Bay.

Continued Threats

Pirate Bay continues to face charges in other countries for breaking copyright laws. But because their servers are located in many places, and the ownership of the company is always under question, the founders of Pirate Bay have often been able to avoid sentencing.

CYBERTERRORISM

Terrorism is one the greatest concerns for governments around the world. The activities of terrorist groups have led to a greater use of security in public places such as airports and railway stations. It has also led to governments passing laws that make it easier to capture terrorists. It is well known that terrorist groups use the Internet to keep in touch with each other and to spread propaganda, but many people are concerned about terrorists using the Internet to attack their enemies.

Defining Cyberterrorism

There is some debate about what cyberterrorism actually is. A narrow definition would be when a known terrorist organization, such as al-Qaeda, uses the Internet to attack a particular target in order to spread panic and alarm. There is also a broader definition which states that any attack using the Internet and has a political or religious goal should be seen as cyberterrorism. Using this last definition makes cyberterrorism a much larger problem, since it can include an individual working by themselves rather than an organization. If the narrow definition is used, then many experts have stated that there have been no known examples of cyberterrorism yet.

ON TARGET

Concerned that their country's computer systems may not be ready to meet a cyberterrorist attack, the United States government has taken steps to confront the situation. The Federal Emergency Management Agency (FEMA) has set up a group called the Cyberterrorism Defense Anlaysis Center. This group provides training for computer experts from government bodies around the country in order to prepare for a large-scale cyberterrorist attack.

◀ A blackened car is taken away from the scene of a bomb blast at Navarra University in Spain. The attack was blamed on the Basque Separatist Group Eta. Eta, like other terrorist groups, uses bomb attacks as well as the Internet to focus attention on its message.

Types of Attacks

Cyberterrorists have a variety of tools that can be used to further their political and religious goals. Hackers involved in this kind of activity are called "hacktivists." If they are able to hack into a web site, then they can change the contents of that site. This can discredit those that they view as their enemies and also help to spread their own messages. Denial-of-service attacks have been known to be used by groups to bring down the web sites of those that they disagree with.

If the denial-of-service attack is successful, then it also means that the victims of those attacks find it difficult to communicate with each other.

▲ An explosion rips through a building during the 1998 attacks on Serbia.

Cyberterrorism in Action

In 1998, NATO countries started bombing selected targets within Serbia in Eastern Europe. The Serbian government was involved in a struggle with a part of Serbia called Kosovo that wanted to split from Serbia. NATO was trying to stop the Serbian government from continuing this conflict. During the NATO bombing, the Chinese Embassy was hit by a bomb, causing a lot of controversy. In May of that year, hackers attacked several U.S. government web sites and left messages protesting the bombing. Nobody is sure if the hackers came from China or Serbia. Eight years later, in 2007, the web site of the former Ukrainian President Victor Yushchenko was attacked by hackers. They defaced the web site and temporarily brought it down. A Russian nationalist group claimed responsibility.

◀ The web site of the former Ukrainian President Victor Yushchenko (left) was targeted by hackers in 2007. He is shown shaking hands with former NATO Secretary General Jaap de Hoop Scheffer.

CYBER WARS

Modern warfare is highly technical. From deciding on troop movements to "smart" weapons that can be guided precisely, technology plays a central role. Computer networks at the heart of operations can be open to attack from cyber warriors—the computer hackers who launch the attacks. If successful, these attacks can give one side of a conflict an advantage by disrupting the computers of the enemy.

Cyber War Methods

In order to bring down a computer network, one side of a conflict could start a denial-of-service attack. This would have the effect of bringing down an entire computer system. Armies would be unable to keep in contact with each other and would lose contact with what was happening on the battlefield. Hackers can also plant malware into the computers of enemy combatants so that they can find out what the enemy is planning. Propaganda is an important tool in warfare, and web site defacement could also be used in order to discredit an enemy.

Cyber War in Action

During the NATO bombing of Serbia in 1998, the United States military successfully hacked into the computer networks of the Serbian air defense system. They managed to trick the Serbian military

ON TARGET

In 2008, members of NATO set up the Cooperative Cyber Defense Center of Excellence. The organization is based in Estonia and was created so that NATO members can work together if they come under a cyber attack during a NATO conflict. At the moment, eight members of NATO are members of the organization.

into believing that bombing attacks were taking place when, in fact, there were no attacks. In July 2009, government computers in both the United States and South Korea came under a sustained denial-of-service attack. On the first day, the web sites of the Pentagon and the White House were attacked. The next day, it was South Korean government web sites that were targeted, and on the third day both governments had to deal with denial-of-service attacks. It has never been established who was behind the attacks. The finger of suspicion has been pointed at China, North Korea, and even Britain, but no evidence has been found.

◀ A U.S. Airforce F-14 Tomcat jet, like this one was used by the U.S. military in the air attacks on Serbia. False information spread by the U.S. military during the 1998 bombing meant that the Serbian authorities were unable to tell whether bombing attacks were about to take place or not.

▲ *Since the first Operation Cyber Storm in 2006, the Department of Homeland Security now runs the same exercise every two years. They are all run from this operations room and involve nearly every government department in the United States.*

▼ *The Department of Homeland Security was created in November 2002 by President George W. Bush. Its job is to protect the United States from terrorist attacks both at home and abroad.*

Operation Cyber Storm

In February 2006, the Department of Homeland Security in the United States ran an exercise called Operation Cyber Storm. They wanted to know how ready government computer networks were in the event of a cyber attack. Security officials from Britain, Canada, Australia, and New Zealand also took part in the exercise. The simulated attack included cyber warriors targeting transportation and communication systems and the energy supply to computers. The exercise revealed that several computer systems were vulnerable to attack and that a coordinated response to any attack was needed.

CASE STUDY: CYBER WARS IN EASTERN EUROPE

Two of the best-known examples of cyber warfare have taken place in Eastern Europe. Both of them involve a dispute between Russia and another country that lies on its borders. The first was in 2007 when there was a disagreement with Estonia over a war memorial. The second example was in 2008 during the South Ossetia conflict in Georgia.

Moving a Statue

In April 2007, the Estonian government decided to relocate a Soviet World War II memorial statue from its position in the capital city, Tallinn, to a cemetery. The already tense relationship between Estonia, once part of the Soviet Union, and Russia quickly blew up into a huge political fight. On the streets of Tallinn, crowds of Russian nationalists protested against the relocation, which they felt to be an insult to Russian soldiers who had died during the conflict.

▶ The Bronze Soldier of Tallinn was unveiled in September 1947 and commemorates the Russian soldiers who died fighting the Nazis in Estonia. For many native Estonians, the statue represented Russian control of their country.

The Attack Begins

On April 27, several Estonian government web sites came under attack. Some of the attacks were by hackers who defaced the web sites, while others were engaged in denial-of-service attacks. It was clear that the attacks were both large-scale and coordinated, but it was not clear who was responsible for the attacks. The Estonian government believed that the Russian government at least supported the cyber attack, but it had no evidence to prove it.

Cyberwar in Georgia

Like Estonia, Georgia was part of the Soviet Union until it became independent in 1991. One part of Georgia, called South Ossetia, wanted to separate and form their own country. In August 2008, the Georgian government tried to regain control of South Ossetia using military force. They were met by South Ossetian troops and also by Russian troops. The presence of Russian armed forces meant that Georgia was unable to continue with the conflict, and a cease fire was agreed upon.

As part of the conflict, both Russian and Georgian web sites were hacked into and defaced. Three days before the Georgian attack, Russian news web sites were hacked into, and the content was replaced with content from a Georgian television station. Georgian web sites were also attacked. The web sites of the Georgian Parliament and the Ministry of Foreign Affairs were changed so that pictures of the Georgian president were replaced with images of Adolf Hitler. There were also denial-of-service attacks on several Georgian web sites, including the official news agency site. Both the Russian and Georgian governments denied any involvement in these cyber attacks.

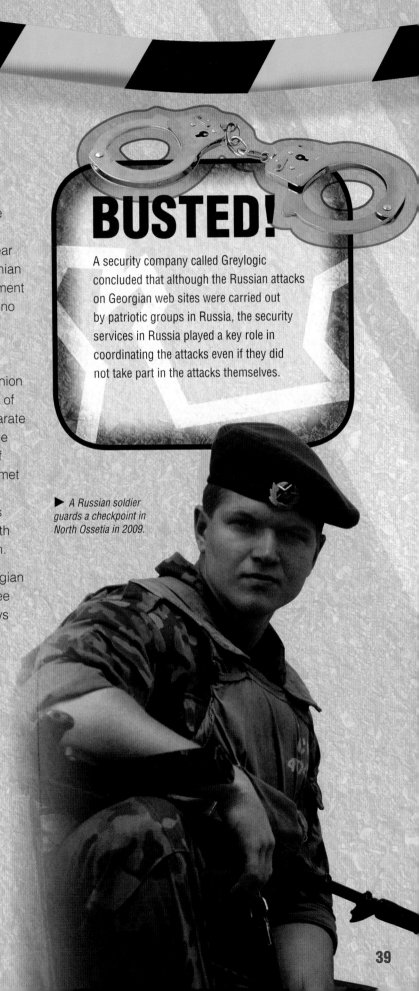

BUSTED!

A security company called Greylogic concluded that although the Russian attacks on Georgian web sites were carried out by patriotic groups in Russia, the security services in Russia played a key role in coordinating the attacks even if they did not take part in the attacks themselves.

▶ A Russian soldier guards a checkpoint in North Ossetia in 2009.

CYBERSECURITY

The rise of different types of cyber crime has meant that both businesses and governments are searching for ways to combat it. The international nature of cyber crime means that different governments and police departments have to work together in order to both prevent cyber crime and to capture those who they believe are guilty of carrying out cyber crimes.

MIGRATION AND CUSTOMS E
CYBER CRIMES CENTER
C³

◀ Don Daufenback, a special agent working for the U.S. Immigration and Customs Enforcement Agency, poses outside the Cyber Crimes Center where he works. This part of the Agency works to prevent illegal activities on the Internet.

ON TARGET

If cyber criminals are to be caught, then police departments need to move fast. The FBI has Cyber Action Teams (CATs). These are highly-trained agents who are ready to act quickly and respond to a developing cyber crime. They work with law enforcement agencies in countries around the world to catch anybody involved in cyber crime.

Homeland Security

In early 2008, President George W. Bush created the Comprehensive National Cybersecurity Initiative as part of the Department of Homeland Security. The job of this group was to improve the security of government computer networks. The group was kept a secret until October 2008 when the government revealed some details about its work. National security reasons were given for this secrecy. When Barack Obama became president in 2008, he appointed Melissa Hathaway to oversee cybersecurity across all the departments of the United States government.

Tackling Cyber Crime

In the United States, the job of tackling cyber crime is shared between the Department of Justice and the FBI. FBI agents are involved in tracking down and closing fraudulent web sites, breaking into the computers of known hackers, and dealing with cyberstalkers. They do not operate by themselves, but work in coordination with police departments and other security agencies in the United States.

Many other countries also have departments dedicated to tackling cyber crime. In Britain, the Police National E-Crime Unit is responsible for coordinating police investigations into cyber crimes. They often work with other police forces and government agencies to combat crimes online.

Business Responses

Businesses around the world have spent millions to defend themselves against cyber crime. Sophisticated firewalls make it much more difficult for hackers to get into a computer network or to install a virus or a piece of malware. However, there is no such thing as a perfect computer security system, and cyber criminals will continue to search for weaknesses in these systems. If a weakness is found, then the security becomes useless and must be replaced. This means that the fight against cyber crime can never really stop.

BUSTED!

In 2006, members of an FBI Cyber Action Team began an investigation into a virus called "Zotob." They traced the origins of the virus back to Turkey and Morocco. Both countries agreed to allow a Cyber Action Team in to find out who had created the virus. Once this had been discovered, the local police took over and arrested several people. The arrests took place only eight days after the virus first started spreading on the Internet.

▼ *Tackling cyber crime has become a profitable business. There are many companies that offer protection from cyber attacks to both governments and businesses. It is estimated that about 8 percent of all computer budgets is spent on security.*

GLOSSARY

adware a piece of software that automatically displays advertisements on a computer; adware can also track which web sites a computer user visits and send that information back to the adware creator.

BitTorrent a way for people to share files over the Internet by allowing people to download files from one computer while simultaneously uploading parts of the same files to somebody else; this allows very large files to easily pass over the Internet.

black hat hackers hackers who hack into computer systems or web sites either to commit a crime or to deface a web site

blog a type of web site regularly updated with someone's personal thoughts

denial-of-service attack a web site attack that works by coordinating a large number of information requests at the same time so that the site either slows down or crashes completely

encryption a way of protecting sensitive information by changing it using a special code that can only be broken if the key to that code is known

extradition an official process when one country asks another country to send them somebody that they believe has committed a crime

file-sharing site web sites that allow users to share music and video files with each other without anything being downloaded from the web site itself

firewall a piece of software that acts as a security system for computers by inspecting all pieces of information that enter or leave a computer

gray hat hackers hackers who sometimes hack into computers sometimes in order to commit a crime and sometimes with no intention of doing harm

hacking to gain unauthorized access to another computer system to find information, change information, or change the appearance of a web site

hacktivists hackers whose motivation is to further a particular political cause

malware a piece of software that hides in a computer; malware can do damage or gather information to be sent to the creator of the malware.

nationalist someone with strong feelings about the country of their birth

network a group of computers that are linked together so that they can share information

packet sniffers small pieces of malware that are used to inspect the information that is being sent along a computer network; when they detect an important piece of information, such as a password, they record and send off that information.

phishing a way of trying to fool people into revealing valuable information, such as bank account details, through e-mail or through web sites

social networking sites web sites that allow groups of people to communicate with each other; popular social networking sites are Facebook, Bebo, MySpace, and Twitter.

spyware a piece of software that keeps track of how somebody uses a computer and then sends that information off to the creator of the spyware

trojan horse a piece of software that pretends to be useful to the user, but once it is used, can cause harm to the user's computer

virus small pieces of software that attach themselves to another piece of software, such as word-processing software, in order to run

white hat hacker a type of hacker who does not have a criminal motivation; he or she may be looking for information or might just enjoy the challenge of getting past computer security systems.

FURTHER INFORMATION

Books

Parks, Peggy J. *Computer Hacking (Crime Scene Investigations),* Lucent Books, 2008.

Townsend, John. *Cyber Crime Secrets (Amazing Crime Scene Science),* Amicus, 2012.

Stefoff, Rebecca. *Cybercrime (Forensic Science Investigated),* Marshall Cavendish Benchmark, 2009.

Web Sites

Sites relating to the fight against cyber crime.

www.fbi.gov/fbikids.htm
The children's section of the FBI web site has some information about how the FBI deals with cyber crime.

Sites offering education, advice, or help.

www.stopbullyingnow.hrsa.gov/kids
Learn all about bullying and what you can do to stop it. Find games and cartoon Webisodes that help you Take a Stand. Lend a Hand. Stop Bullying Now!

www.cybercitizenship.org/crime/crime.html
This web site has information on how schools can teach students about cyber crime and how to behave properly when on the Internet.

www.getnetwise.org
This web site has useful information on how people can protect themselves from cyber criminals while they are using the Internet.

www.ftc.gov/bcp/edu/microsites/idtheft/index.html
This web site is a one-stop national resource to learn about the crime of identity theft. It provides detailed information to help you deter, detect, and defend against identity theft.

www.justice.gov/criminal/cybercrime/rules/lessonplan1.htm
A web site from the U.S. Department of Justice that gives teachers ideas about how to teach young people about cyber crime.

www.netsmartz.org/index.aspx
A site dedicated to providing educational resources to parents, teachers, and students to teach others how to be safe on the Internet.

Note to parents and teachers: Every effort has been made by the publishers to ensure that these web sites are suitable for children, that they are of the highest educational value, and that they contain no inappropriate or offensive material. However, because of the nature of the Internet, it is impossible to guarantee that the contents of these sites will not be altered. We strongly advise that Internet access is supervised by a responsible adult.

INDEX

SERIES CONTENTS